Princes of the Antarctic,
emperor penguins
survive in extreme conditions

The penguin's wings are well adapted for swimming.

LEGIONS FACE THE WIND

In the depths of the antarctic winter, ice-laden winds can reach speeds of up to 300 kilometres per hour across the ice floes. The feeble rays of the sun, which appears for only a few hours each day, are not enough to stop the temperature from dropping to –50°C. To protect themselves against the biting cold, the emperor penguins form a circle, like the 'tortoise' formation used by the Roman legions of antiquity. In this formation a few individuals protect the others from the prevailing winds and because the circle rotates no single penguin remains exposed for long.

Emperor penguins congregate in colonies of between 300 and 100,000 individuals. To protect themselves from the cold they split into small groups and adopt a 'tortoise' formation. When their feathers become covered in ice, the penguins on the edge of the circle move into the centre to warm themselves through contact with their fellows.

A procession of emperor penguins.

Profile

Emperor penguins

Aptenodytes forsteri
Family: pheniscidae
Class: birds

Size: 1 – 1.20 m
Weight: 30 – 40 kg
Distribution: Antarctica; breeds on the coastal ice floes, feeds at sea
Diet: fish, shellfish, molluscs, cephalopods
Number of eggs: one per couple
Incubation and rearing period: 62 – 65 days incubating the egg; 150 days rearing chicks
Life expectancy: more than 30 years

GENERAL MEETING ON THE ICE

At the start of the Antarctic winter the emperor penguins leave the ocean that feeds them and gather on the ice. Each colony, consisting on average of 3000 individuals, then begins a long migration to its usual breeding ground. The birds set off in single file, waddling on their sturdy feet at speeds of 1 – 2 kilometres per hour, sliding downhill on their bellies whenever they can. After travelling tens of kilometres, they split into pairs before beginning their mating display. In April or May, when the temperature is around –40°C, the female lays a single egg which she immediately shelters in her 'incubator' (see box). After a few hours she passes it over to her mate and returns to the shore to feed. The male sits on the egg for over two months, keeping it at a temperature of 34°C. When the egg hatches in July, the female returns to take over from the male, who will have lost 40% of his body weight in his long fast.

A well heated incubator

Emperor penguins keep their eggs and chicks wrapped up warmly between their abdomen and their feet. When the adult squats, it exposes skin richly served by blood vessels. When an egg or chick is resting on the adult's feet, these blood vessels come into contact with the egg. A roll of feather-covered skin then entirely covers the egg and the penguin's feet, thus creating an individually heated 'incubator'.

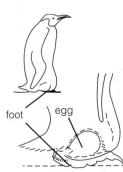

foot   egg

Comfortably settled on its mother's feet, the chick is oblivious to the cold snow. When the wind blows it shelters in its snug 'incubator'.

Gradually the chicks become more independent.

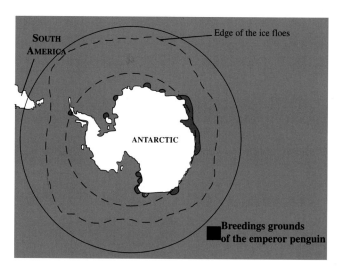

SOUTH AMERICA

Edge of the ice floes

ANTARCTIC

■ Breedings grounds of the emperor penguin

CHICKS GO TO THE CRECHE

The female feeds her chick by regurgitating food that she has stored in her stomach. In September the chick is big enough and its down is sufficiently thick that it no longer needs the 'incubator'.

It then joins the colony's creche, where all young penguins go. Its parents can now go back and forth between the breeding ground and the ocean where they feed. On each return they feed their own chick, which they identify by its voice.

When they are about 40 days old, the young emperor penguins leave the bosom of the family to gather in creches.
In the chill wind they follow the example of their elders and adopt the 'tortoise' formation.
In this way they use up no more energy when the temperature is −30°C than they would on their own at −5°C.

At the start of the Antarctic winter, the emperor penguin colonies migrate to the breeding grounds in the frozen continent's interior. They cross the slippery ground on their solid feet, using their wings to help them balance. They maintain a firm grip on the hard ice by means of the strong claws on their webbed feet.

Living up to its reputation
red foxes
are cunning hunters

DIFFERENT HUNTING TECHNIQUES

Although red foxes sometimes fill their stomachs with earthworms and different fruits, their main diet consists of small mammals. When this nocturnal hunter decides to catch itself a rabbit, its favourite meal, it lies in wait near a burrow entrance, ready to surprise the occupier. With one snap of its jaws it breaks the neck of its prey, which it devours on the spot or drags back to its own earth. To catch small rodents, however, the fox uses the 'mousing' method. Here the fox slips smoothly and lightly through the grass, listening for the slightest sound. By moving its ears it can determine the precise locations of any fieldmice or voles scurrying nearby. With one strong, deft movement it leaps a metre into the air, stretching out its tail and slightly bending its front legs, then lands on its prey, breaking the rodent's spine. The agile fox repeats these movements over and over with amazing success.

Profile

Red foxes
Vulpes vulpes
Family: canidae
Class: mammals
Weight: 6 – 7 kg
Size: total length 1.25 m tail about 45 cm
Distribution: North America, Europe, North Africa, Middle East, Asia Minor, Central Asia, Siberia, Japan, China, Northern India and Indochina, Australia.
Habitat: forest, fields, grassland, tundra, mountains, shoreline, semi-desert, towns
Diet: omnivorous
Life expectancy: 4 years (may be as long as 12 years)

The red fox is a cunning hunter who knows how to hide, even when on the move. Crossing this open field it proceeds with caution, keeping its body close to the ground and its ears pointing forwards.

Red foxes eat all kinds of foods in the course of their adventures, from blackberries and insects to frogs and rodents. Although rabbits are their favourite meal, they sometimes catch birds that nest on the ground, such as this pheasant. Such fine prey will attract other envious creatures, so the hunter drags it back to its earth.

Furnished accommodation

Red foxes do not like hard work and prefer to take over a pre-dug earth rather than make their own. If they have to get their paws dirty, they settle for one tunnel and a single room. However when a fox 'rents' a place, it generally digs out dead-end tunnels to use as hiding-places for when it is being chased.

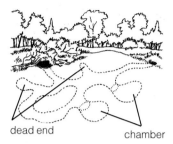

dead end   chamber

YET THEY SURVIVE

Humans dislike foxes because they attack their poultry. They are hunted down and killed for sport or for their fur. Sometimes they are exterminated because they carry rabies. Nevertheless, the red fox survives throughout the northern hemisphere. When towns spread into the surrounding countryside, turning fields and woods into urban parks, some foxes are able to adapt to this new setting. They feed at night, scavenging on dumps and in dustbins left out by human beings. The remarkable ease with which these urban foxes seem able to adapt to city life is particularly apparent in London, where they became frequent visitors to Trafalgar Square in the 1970s.

The fox's ability to adapt fits perfectly with its reputation for being cunning, which has followed it since antiquity. Back in the sixth century BC Aesop's fables portrayed the fox as the craftiest animal, a symbol which then spread throughout medieval Europe. In Japan its image is used to bring prosperity.

Red foxes are not home-loving creatures. They use their earths only as shelter from bad weather, a place to eat large prey or to give birth. Very young cubs are allowed to play in a nest near the entrance to the earth. As they become older, they become used to going further from home.

Red foxes are omnivores who adapt their tastes to suit the food available in their environment.
Since there are not many rabbits in the marshy Camargue region in the south of France,
the fox will happily dive into a pool to catch a nice fresh fish.

Though lacking any natural defences
grass snakes
make an impression on their enemies

The grass snake has large scales on its head.

A GREAT ACTOR

The grass snake is totally harmless, as it has no deadly venom. Instead, when it senses danger, it uses a sophisticated trick to make its predators think twice. First it vomits up its food and empties its intestines, then its body begins to tremble, after which it turns over, opens its mouth and lets its tongue hang out, so that the attacker thinks it is dead.

This reptile, can grow up to two metres long, and is found in Europe, north-west Africa and western Asia. It prefers damp places, where it catches frogs, toads and tritons.

With its head hanging, mouth open and tongue hanging out, the grass snake looks completely dead.
The fetid smell of its vomit adds to the disguise. However, if the attacker tries to turn the snake's head back the right way up, it stops acting at once and tries to escape.

The grass snake is found throughout Europe. Its colour, varies between green and brown and provides it with effective camouflage in the damp meadows, marshes, ditches, pools and rivers that are its preferred habitat. Grass snakes are excellent swimmers and live close to water in which they hunt and sometimes hide.

To cut up their prey
red-backed shrikes
use meat hooks

Red-backed shrikes nest in thorny hedges, so they have all the stakes they need for impaling their prey.

IMPALED TO DEATH

With its one foot and 35 centimetre wingspan the red-backed shrike seems half-size compared to eagles and vultures, yet this little bird proves itself to be alarmingly fierce when devouring other creatures. In particular insects are first impaled on thorns or on barbed wire, after which the cruel executioner attacks them with its beak before enjoying the tender flesh of its victims. The red-backed shrike also uses thorny bushes as larders where it impales a number of insects.

Natural larding-pins

Perched in a thorny shrub, this male is taking the outer casing off an insect it has just caught. It tears off the carapace with its hooked beak, using the long, sharp thorns to help it, just as a butcher uses long needles called larding pins to hold and manipulate meat.

Profile

Red-backed shrikes
Lanius collurio
Family: lanidae
Class: birds

Size: about 18 cm
Habitat: sunlit hedges and bushes
Migration: at the end of August these birds leave Europe for southern Africa
Number of eggs: 5 – 6

Before building their nest, these young parents have carefully and patiently removed the thorns from the area, in order to avoid suffering the same fate as their prey.

Red-backed shrikes readily attack large prey. This male has just carried a small mammal to its 'larder' where, after sticking it on to the thorns, it will cut it to pieces using the hook at the end of its powerful beak. This feeding habit has given the shrike a reputation among human beings as a blood-thirsty sadist.

With agile fingers and large heads
chimpanzees
are the most gifted inhabitant of the savannah woodlands

CUDDLES CEMENT THE GROUP

From birth onwards the young chimpanzee clings to its mother's belly, where it has both food and protection. At the age of one it can hold on to her back to travel. During its youth and until it becomes an adult at the age of 13, the young chimpanzee learns to find its own food, travel and communicate with the other group members by playing with its mother. These games develop the young animal's muscles and teach it the rules of group life. As it grows it develops a full range of cries, postures and mimicry.

A STICK FOR EATING ANTS

Chimpanzees are omnivorous and like to include insects such as ants on their menu. When a chimp feels like eating some of these little delicacies, it looks for a big ants' nest, then finds a thin branch of up 60 centimetres long and carefully removes all the leaves to make a straight stick. The chimp then

Profile

Chimpanzee
Pan troglodytes
Order: primates
Class: mammals

Size: male: 75 – 95 cm
female: 70 – 85 cm
Weight: male: 40 kg (in the wild)
female: 30 kg (in the wild)
Habitat: damp forest, dry forest, mountain forest and savannah woodland
Diet: mainly fruit and insects; may sometimes eat leaves and small mammals
Life expectancy: 40 – 45 years

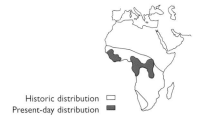

Young chimpanzees very rarely leave their mother. They exchange caresses or have play fights, strengthening their bond and the little one's muscles. Later the young chimp will leave his mother from time to time to go and play with others of his own age.

plunges this stick into the ants' nest. To fight off the intruder the ants rush on to the stick and bite into it with their jaws. Then all the chimp needs to do is take the stick out of the nest and run it between its lips for a delicious snack. Chimps can adapt their tool to suit the food they desire: to attack a termites' nest, whose walls are stronger than those of an ants' nest, they find a less flexible stick.

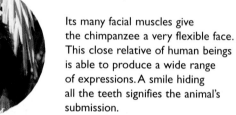

This chimpanzee is making a tool from a twig.

Its many facial muscles give the chimpanzee a very flexible face. This close relative of human beings is able to produce a wide range of expressions. A smile hiding all the teeth signifies the animal's submission.

For monkeys that live in groups, caresses and other forms of physical contact are a regular part of group life. Grooming is not only a matter of hygiene, picking the parasites from another group member's fur, but also a ritual that strengthens emotional bonds and hierarchies. Chimpanzees also communicate through grimaces, posture, gestures and cries.

Chimpanzees feed mainly on leaves and fruits. Sometimes they may supplement their diet with a little meat, in the form of small mammals or, more usually, insects. Besides ants and termites, which they catch in their nests, they also dig out insect larvae which grow under tree bark.

To camouflage themselves
cuttlefish
have plenty of tricks

Cuttlefish live among the rocks in the sandy shallows.

Like other members of its family, the squid and the octopus, the cuttlefish has very keen eyesight. Its eyes have a cornea, an iris, a crystalline lens, a retina and two eyelids. However, it cannot see in colour.

A CLOUD OF INK

When looking for a small crab or a tasty shrimp to relieve its hunger, the cuttlefish often meets other, more dangerous creatures, particularly when it is rummaging about among the rocks, a favourite place for sharp-toothed conger eels. To escape this greedy fish the cuttlefish uses an ingenious ploy: it squirts out a cloud of ink before escaping to shelter. The enemy is thus confronted by a thick, dark screen and loses sight of its snack.

The ink is made and stored in an organ known as the 'ink sac'. When the cuttlefish is frightened the ink is squirted out by a powerful jet of water and forms a thick cloud. It is a very dark substance and was formerly used in China for the manufacture of writing ink.

Frightened by a predator's presence, the cuttlefish instantly changes colour. As it grows paler it squirts out a powerful jet of water and ink which shoots it backwards. The enemy is initially blinded by the ink cloud, after which substances within the cloud disturb its sense of smell, so that it loses all track of its victim.

Profile

Common cuttlefish
Sepia officinalis
Class: cephalopods
Order: decapods
Branch: molluscs

Size: up to 65 cm including tentacles of 30 cm
Distribution: Atlantic, Mediterranean
Habitat: coastal waters
Diet: shellfish, fish
Number of eggs: about 500 lemon-shaped eggs, in black clusters
Predators: small sharks, ray, hake, conger eel, dolphin, seal, birds

Before catching a crab, the cuttlefish adopts an attacking position. It raises its tentacles and leaps on top of its prey, which it grabs from behind, before devouring it with its powerful beak.

CAMOUFLAGE CHAMPION

When it does not want to be seen, the cuttlefish changes its skin colour. Like the chameleon, it can imitate the colours of its environment at will. This is particularly useful when the cuttlefish is lying in wait for crabs. It burrows a little way into the sand of the sea bed and makes its skin turn pale and speckled with brown. The crab is then unable to see the cuttlefish, which seems to be no more than a bump on the sea bed. The cuttlefish allows the imprudent crab to pass by, then jumps on it from behind in order to avoid being painfully caught in its pincers. Holding the crab by means of suckers on its legs, the cuttlefish devours its prey.

AN EAGER PUPIL

The cuttlefish has an amazing capacity to learn. Once it has been injured by a crab's pincers when attacking from the front, the young cuttlefish learns and remembers that it is much safer to attack from behind.

Instant suntan

For camouflage, or during courtship displays, the cuttlefish changes colour by altering the appearance of the coloured patches on its skin. These patches are in fact tiny sacs (chromatophores)

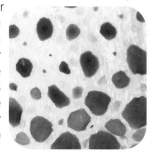

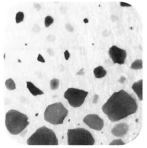

containing pigments of different colours. By dilating or contracting particular kinds of sac the cuttlefish can selectively change colour to blend in with the background.

The empty sea bed? Not exactly... a cuttlefish is hiding in the centre. Buried under a thin layer of sand, whose colours it has imitated, it would be invisible if its eyes did not give it away.

Perfect parents,
Sexton beetles
bury dead bodies for their young

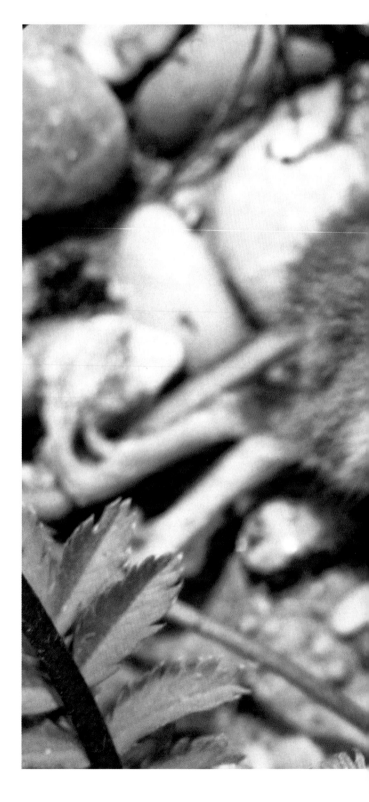

HIDING THE BODY

During the reproductive period, sexton beetles (whose zoological name necrophorus comes from the Greek meaning 'carrier of the dead') are obsessed with one thing: finding the fresh corpse of a bird or small mammal. When it does so the beetle drives off the small insects which have already been drawn to the body, then seeks out a place where the earth is soft to bury its loot. It returns to the dead animal and slides underneath it with its back to the ground. By moving its legs, it gradually transports the body. When it is joined by a beetle of the opposite sex, it buries the corpse. The young couple then construct a comfortable underground chamber around the body, from which they take hairs or feathers. After mating, the female lays her eggs in a narrow corridor, then organises food distribution by taking little pieces of flesh from the corpse for the larvae to feed on during the early stages of their development.

Profile

Sexton beetles
Family: silphidae
Class: insects
Order: coleoptera

Size: 10 – 30 mm
Habitat: forest floor and meadows
Diet: dead bodies of small mammals, birds or batrachians
Social structure: live in pairs at the time of reproduction
Social behaviour: the larvae are fed by their parents until they pupate
Noted as: an investigatory aid in forensic medicine

Sexton beetles play an important part in the decomposition of animal flesh. In the 19th century police scientists became interested in their behaviour as a means of determining the date of death of bodies found in the countryside.

The sexton beetle's acute sense of smell enables it to detect a dead animal up to about one kilometre away. After driving away its rivals, it goes in search of a place where the ground is soft and begins to dig a hole to bury the corpse. Then it alternates between moving the body and enlarging its tunnel.

For better fishing
humpback whales
spread a net of bubbles

FANTASTIC FISHING

Humpback whales are found in all of the world's oceans. Each year they migrate between the polar regions, where they feed, and the tropical zones, where they reproduce. They return to the cold polar waters after a starvation diet lasting about six months, arriving at the time when the days are lengthening and the water and air are getting warmer. This warming stimulates a rapid increase in the numbers of plankton, krill (small shellfish) and fish on which the whales feed. When the whales need to feed they dive for between 5 and 20 minutes to depths of between 60 and 180 metres. They catch their prey by swallowing enormous

A whale caught while making a spectacular leap.

Humpback whales gather in the cold waters of Alaska, which are rich in food. The group then fishes together. They form a circle under a shoal of krill and 'spread' their net of bubbles which traps their prey. The group then moves up, following the trapped shellfish. On the surface these giants can then greedily tuck into their catch.

quantities of water and can change the volume of each mouthful using their deep, wide ventral folds or furrows. The stomachs of these insatiable animals can hold 600 herrings and 700 kilograms of cod and plankton.

MR AND MRS WHALE ON THEIR HONEYMOON

At the end of the feeding period the whales leave the polar waters for the warm seas of the tropics. Gestating females leave last so that they can take the greatest advantage of the abundant food in the polar region. After travelling nearly 6000 kilometres, singly or in small groups,

The net of bubbles

To feed, the humpback whale dives under a shoal of krill, then spirals back up to the surface, expelling air. The bubbles form a net

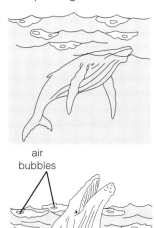

air bubbles

which imprisons the crustaceans. Once on the surface the whale opens its mouth and swallows up to 6 cubic metres of water, which it then expels by pushing its tongue against its palate.

Several tonnes of krill are thus caught in the filter formed by the whalebone plates. To increase the efficiency of this procedure whales sometimes form groups, thereby increasing the diameter of their net of bubbles.

The whale's trap is effective. Its whalebone plates (the dark slats) cover the opening of its enormous mouth and when the whale expels the water full of krill by moving its tongue, the shellfish are held prisoner inside this filter. Seabirds catch the small fish that escape, taking care not to get caught themselves.

Profile

Humpback whale
Megaptera novaeangliae
Class: mammals
Order: cetacea
Suborder: mysticeteae

Size: 15 m
Weight: 30 tonnes
Birthweight: 900 – 1200 kg
Diet: krill, small fish
Gestation period: 11 – 12 months
Suckling period: 10 – 11 months
Life expectancy: 30 years
Social structure: solitary or in small, temporary groupings of two to ten individuals

they congregate in the breeding grounds. A group of up to 12 individuals forms temporarily around a central female accompanied by an adult male. In order to retain his place as protector, this male drives away other males who approach the female. He acts aggressively and may even charge his rivals when simple intimidation fails.

WARM WATER BIRTH

In the tropics the humpback whales choose shallow coastal waters, varying in temperature between 22 and 25°C. While the dominant males court the females that are on heat, other females are preparing to give birth. The baby whale weighs about one tonne and is about 4.5 metres long. As soon as it is born, it makes its way to its mother's teats and sucks hungrily. It swallows about 12 litres of very rich milk at each feed, representing a daily total of 500 litres.

Humpback whales dive only occasionally, for example when searching for food. On the surface they carry out manoeures, as though performing a delicate ballet. They skim the surface or strike it with their pectoral fins or tail, their movements are surprisingly graceful for animals of such a size.

Young humpback whales spend most of their time playing acrobatic water games. This behaviour, very common between the ages of one and four, ends when the animal turns five. However, males later use some of the same movements in the mating season. Here a young male practices 'breaching', in which he shoots vertically out of the water.

Before the cold season
moles
stock the larder

Moles have very weak eyesight. These small insectivores find their prey using their senses of smell and touch.

WORMS IN RESERVE

The common mole digs an underground network of tunnels, making its home at the centre of the tunnel system. Several times a day it passes through these tunnels looking for the earthworms and insect larvae it likes to eat. However, since worms are scarce in winter, the greedy mole stocks up in autumn. To do this, it digs a second well in which it piles its still-living prey, having taken care to disable the worms by biting them so that they cannot escape.

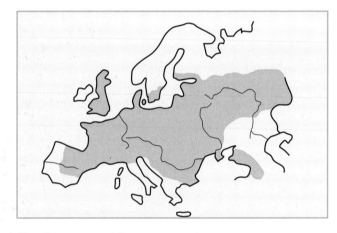

Distribution map of the common mole

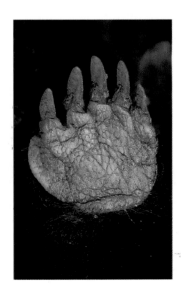

The mole's front paws are excellent digging tools. In one movement it digs with its claws and scoops the dug earth back towards its hind legs with its palms.

Fields frequented by moles are easy to spot from the little mounds of earth, called molehills, formed during the animals' excavations.

TRENCH WARFARE

Moles are unsociable animals whose behaviour is often aggressive. The soft rich earth of meadows often attracts several moles, who occupy the same space but carefully avoid meeting. In the mating season, however, males often venture into neighbouring tunnels in search of a female. If, during the visit, the adventurer comes face to face with another male, a fight ensues. The combatants exchange violent blows while warbling loudly. The winner often feasts on his rival's lacerated remains.

Profile

Common mole
Talpa europaea
Family: talpidae
Class: mammals
Order: insectivores

Size: 11 – 17 cm (plus 2 – 3.5 cm for the tail); male larger than female
Weight: 65 – 120 g
Habitat: 10 – 60 cm underground; mainly in fields, pasture and deciduous forest
Diet: carnivorous; earthworms, insect larvae, sometimes woodlice, spiders, batrachians, mice
Number of young per litter: 3 – 4 on average (once a year)
Life expectancy: 3 – 4 years

The mole grasps one end of the earthworm in its teeth and pulls it through its front claws to clean off the soil. It can then eat it without the risk of breaking a tooth. This technique also allows the mole to empty the worm's intestine, which is full of earth and abrasive minerals.

Strength in numbers for
white pelicans
living in non-hierarchical communities

For white pelicans there is no alternative to group life. Each individual constantly seeks out the company of its fellows, whether for preening, walking around, resting on the water, swimming or reproducing. For nesting, pelicans choose places near to stretches of water, where they may gather in flocks of several thousand.

LONG LIVE THE GROUP!

Pelicans live in groups, which may vary in size from ten or so to several thousand individuals. There is no hierarchy in the group: each bird carries out all the activities of the species in the company of its fellows, from fishing and travelling to resting and even reproduction.

This arrangement has two advantages: firstly, a compact group can defend itself more easily against predators than an isolated individual and the chances of noticing an enemy in the vicinity increase with the size of the group. Secondly, when fishing pelicans surround their prey thereby increasing their catch.

Pelicans like to sit in the treetops. They wait in their observation posts until it is time to fish, benefiting from the comparative coolness of their perch. They may sometimes take a few twigs to strengthen their nests, which are built on the ground.

Synchronised fishing in a fish-filled lake.

FISHING WITH A NET

The pelican eats only fish, which it generally takes from shallow water. It prefers fish that live in shoals, since it has a greater chance of catching one when it plunges its beak into the water. Pelicans fish sometimes alone and sometimes together. When a colony fishes together it descends on a stretch of water then divides into small groups of between 6 and 20 birds. Each group forms a semi-circle and moves slowly forward, carefully studying the water. As soon as they have surrounded a shoal of fish, the birds all plunge their beaks into the water, spreading their wings for balance. A few seconds later the whole group raise their heads with an extraordinary degree of synchronisation.

Once again, all the pelicans benefit from working in a group, since the row of open beaks under the water acts just like a fishing net, from which the shoal of fish has great difficulty escaping.

Ideal fishing tool

When a pelican plunges its beak into the water to catch a fish, the muscles at the base of its tongue stretch along a pouch which hangs down under its beak (the throat pouch). This holds 12 litres on average and is an efficient trap, made more so when the upper part of the beak, which ends in a pointed hook, closes over it like a lid.

Profile

White pelican
Pelecanus onocrotalus
Family: pelicanidae
Class: birds
Wingspan: 2.7 – 3.6 m
Weight: 9 – 11 kg
Distribution: eastern Europe, central Asia, northern India, tropical Africa
Habitat: lakes, seashore, inland marshes
Diet: piscivorous
Incubation period: 29 – 36 days
Number of young: 1 – 3
Sexual maturity: three or four years old
Egg weight: 155 – 195 g
Social structure: gregarious, monogamous

Pelicans living near a lake full of fish arrive at their fishing ground in groups of between five and twenty birds.

Despite its sturdy shape, the pelican flies with ease.

'Pneumatic' bones

The pelican is amazingly light given the fact that it is so fat, and this is what allows it to fly. Its lightness stems from the internal structure of its bones, most of which are hollow. The chambers created contain air rather than denser bony material. Small transverse columns give rigidity and strength to the bones, enabling the support of considerable weights.

ulna

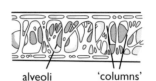

alveoli   'columns'

AND WHAT'S MORE IT FLIES

With an average weight of 10 kilograms, the pelican is one of the heaviest birds capable of flight. During its long migrations it combines wing-beating, which uses up a lot of energy, with gliding, during which it can rest and take advantage of rising currents of warm air. In addition, pelicans fly in a chevron formation to help the group move through the air. The heron and the pelican are the only birds to fly with their necks bent. This enables them to bear the weight of their enormous beaks.

In order to fly, the pelican runs to gather speed until the point where its legs have propelled it fast enough to take off. When landing it breaks by spreading out its wings, tail and webbed feet, which act as air brakes.

The lower half of the pelican's long beak opens into a deep, coloured pouch. The colour of the head and particularly of the beak, throat pouch and area around the eyes indicates the bird's sexual maturity. During the mating season these colours intensify and stimulate displays of courtship.

To fool their enemies
opossums
pretend to be dead

Towards dawn the opossum seeks out a shelter. Depending on its luck, this might be an abandoned burrow, a crevice in a rock or a thick bush among the mangroves. Within five trips the opossum has comfortably furnished its resting place with leaves.

AN OPPORTUNIST WHO LIVES BY NIGHT

The Virginia opossum is a nocturnal animal that waits until dusk before going in search of food. It will eat anything, as long as it is not too hard to catch. During its wanderings it devours insects, earthworms, fruits, leaves, seeds, frogs, rodents, snakes, crayfish and even young opossums.

If it encounters a predator, the opossum lies on its side with its eyes half-closed and its tongue hanging out. The predator is tricked into believing the opossum is already dead and loses interest in what it thinks is a stiffened corpse.

The four-footed opossum is a good walker and an excellent climber.
On sensing danger during its nightly wanderings it takes refuge in the trees,
where its prehensile tail offers it a fifth point of support.

The skin at the end of its long nose is naked and pink.

EVERY ANIMAL FOR ITSELF

Opossums are solitary and aggressive, only tolerating the presence of another opossum during reproductive periods. At this time a male will approach a female cautiously, attracted by her scent. If she is on heat, she will accept his advances, followed by 15 to 20 minutes of mating. As soon as they have finished the now undesirable male is driven away by the female with teeth, claws and cries.

After only 13 days gestation about 20 young are born in an immature state, as is the case with all marsupials. Using the claws on their front feet, the babies, only 15 millimetres long and weighing less than 0.15 grammes, climb up to the marsupial pouch on their mother's belly. As they arrive they each fix on one of their mother's teats, of which there are never more than 17 in total. Those unfortunates that lose their grip on the way, or cannot find one of the ten functioning teats, inevitably die.

A good climber

Using its four feet and prehensile tail, the opossum climbs into the trees, where it often takes refuge. The sharp claws on its front feet dig firmly into the bark, while, with the aid of opposable thumbs without nails, its hind feet grip into the slightest lumps and bumps, and thin branches.

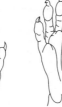

right 'hand'   right foot

The mother opossum carries her babies on her back when they reach three months old. They cling to her fur and wrap their tails round hers.

'Time to eat!' dance
honey bees
in their colony

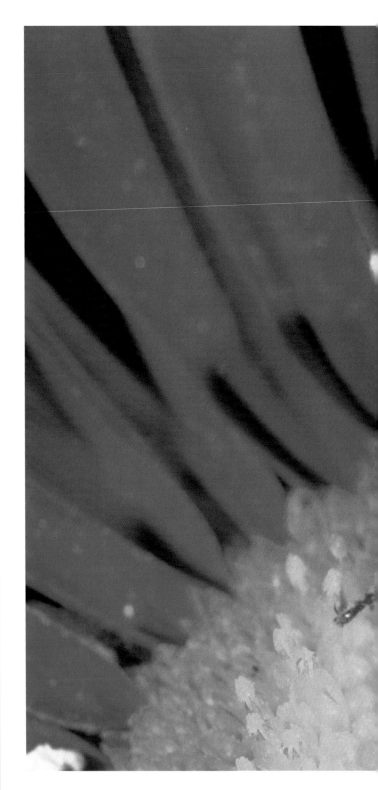

SHARING TASKS

Honey bees, bees that make honey, form colonies within which individual members stick together especially when in danger. The group gathers round a queen, who reproduces and regulates activities. The colony comprises about 2500 males, also known as drones, and about 50,000 female workers.

In each colony the queen is the only one able to lay eggs, producing up to 2000 a day. Moreover, she leads the whole group, giving orders in the form of chemical messages. The drones have one function only: to impregnate the new queen at the time of the nuptial flight. The rest of the work is done by the workers, who perform different tasks according to their age.

MANY JOBS IN A SINGLE LIFE

In the first days of its life the worker bee cleans the empty brood cells. It then becomes a nanny taking care of the larvae. Next it becomes a cleaner (clearing out waste and dead bodies), a builder (making cells) and a storekeeper (storing pollen and nectar in the cells). Before going out to collect nectar it works as a sentinel protecting the nest.

Types of bees

The queen, the drone and the worker are different sizes. The male is characterised by its two very large eyes and square abdomen. The cell in which it develops and those of the workers are hexagonal. The queen, who grows in a vast royal cell, is larger than the workers and feeds throughout her life on royal jelly, which is highly nutritious.

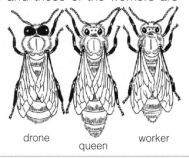

drone

queen

worker

This worker bee collecting pollen has received a little present while visiting a flower. Two stamens laden with pollen grains have become stuck to its head and will disseminate their fertile contents when the bee rubs against another plant.

This worker bee specialising in pollen collection can be identified by the little balls contained in the sacs on its back legs. On returning to the nest, the bee will tell its fellow bees about the new collecting places it has discovered. Guided by the sun's rays, these bees will then come to take the pollen from the ripe stamens.

The eggs are placed vertically in the bottom of the cells, which have first been cleaned by the worker bees. After three days the cells open, each releasing a larva, which then quickly develops.

LIFE AND DEATH OF A QUEEN

At regular intervals in the life of a colony the queen gathers two thirds of the bees into a swarm and flies off with them to form a new colony. The worker bees left in the old colony raise new queens immediately. The first queen to be born kills her rivals by stinging them to death.

Inside her nest, the queen fulfils her reproductive function, laying one egg every 40 seconds. The egg, about 1.5 millimetres in diameter when laid, opens on the third day to release a voracious larva, which sheds its skin four times as it grows before pupating.

Profile

Honey bee
Apis mellifica
Apidae
Hymenoptera
Insects

Distribution: Europe, Africa, Australia
Habitat: any place in which melliferous plants grow
Diet: pollen and nectar
Life expectancy (average): queen: 4 – 5 years; winter worker: 6 months; summer worker: 38 days; drone: 22 days.
Social structure: colonies of several thousand individuals

A DOMESTIC ANIMAL

A colony can make 1 kilogram of honey each day. Human beings have domesticated bees by making hives for them, so obtaining a ready supply of honey that is rich in sugars, vitamins and minerals.

After developing rapidly the larva pupates, and takes on its definitive form.

40

The chrysalis has completed its development. The young bee struggles out of the cell after cutting open the operculum. Recognisable by the long hairs covering its body, it will begin its life as a worker by cleaning out the empty cells.

When the population of a colony grows too large, the queen leaves the nest and gathers a swarm around her. During this time scouts fly off to find a place where a new nest can be built and return to present their findings to the group, using a highly elaborate code. The bees, gorged with honey to cope with this move, then fly off in the direction shown.

The hive entrance is a place of great activity.
All the worker bees, whose job is to collect food, pass through it several times a day and are immediately identified by the guards. These guards keep a close watch in order to stop any intruders from entering.

THE JOB OF THE COLLECTORS

Worker bees in the food-collecting group are highly specialised. Each visits only one type of flower and collects a particular type of food: nectar, pollen, propolis (resin from tree buds) or water. Pollen, an indispensable food for young bees, is produced by the male organs of flowering plants. To collect it, the bee uses its mandibles to tear a stamen from which it removes the pollen grains. These are dampened with honey brought from the nest, which it uses to form the pollen into little balls, these are then placed in the 'sacs' on its back legs.

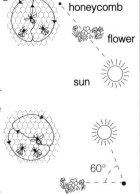

The bees' dance

The collectors' flight on the honeycomb of the hive – the bees' dance – can be interpreted by means of a code. The shape of the dance (circle, semi-circle or figure of eight) indicates how far away the new food source is. The flight's orier in relation to the comb give the angle of the direction to take and the other collectors can even find out how difficult the journey is from the speed of the dance.

If it finds a new source of food, the collector indicates the location to its fellow bees on returning to the colony. It takes up a certain position in relation to the honeycomb and performs a flight which can be decoded to give the direction and distance.

All the work of the hive's society is organised around the queen (centre of the picture), who is longer than the other bees.
She regulates the other bees' tasks by giving them orders in the form of chemical messages (pheromones).
She is the only bee to lay eggs, the workers take care of the larvae and maintain stocks of food.

The collector bee chooses only one species of plant from which to collect. Each time it visits a flower it unintentionally picks up a few pollen grains on its hairs, which then fall off during its visits to other flowers. Thus, by stopping at a number of flowers, bees make an important contribution to the pollination, and thus reproduction of flowers.

In their 'service station'
cleaner fish
offer grooming in exchange for a meal

A large surgeonfish comes to have its wound tended by a cleaner fish, guiding the cleaner to the wound so that it can clean parasites that might cause an infection. The cleaner indicates which part of the body it wants to inspect by tickling it with its caudal fin. The surgeonfish shows its agreement by keeping still but, when it decides the consultation is over, it puts an end to the grooming by moving.

MUTUALLY BENEFICIAL EXCHANGE

In the coral reefs of the Indo-Pacific region cleaner fish set up shop in a particular spot, which scientists call the 'cleaning station'. Here they attract large fish by quivering their tails. If a grouper or surgeonfish needs a bit of grooming, it parks itself in the station. At once the cleaner fish inspects its entire body, eating all the parasites developing on it. The cleaner may even 'clean' its client's teeth, if it finds food remains on them. Thus the large fish delivers a meal to the cleaner at home and, in exchange, receives treatment that prevents the development of skin disease.

This large triggerfish is quite passive in relation to the little cleaner. All the fish of the coral reef know how to find the 'cleaning stations' and view them as zones of non-aggression. Indeed predators and their prey are quite indifferent to each other if they meet while being groomed or queuing for their turn.

The little cleaner is very vulnerable when attached to the fish it is cleaning, since its field of vision is restricted to the latter's gills, mouth or fins. Fortunately, the large fish keeps a close watch on the surrounding area and gives a warning
if it sees a suspicious-looking creature.

To avoid looking after their greedy chicks
common cuckoos
abandon it in another bird's nest

Before laying an egg the female cuckoo looks for a nest to exploit, preferably of the same species as her own adoptive parents. She often chooses the nest of a meadow titlark, sedge warbler, accentor, robin, wagtail or wren. The cuckoo's egg is a similar colour to those already in the nest, but is larger in size.

UNFIT MOTHER

In the mating season the male attracts the female's attention with his 'cuckoo' calls. When a fine female arrives, the seducer offers her a blade of grass as a love token.

The pair do not build a nest. Instead, when time comes to lay, the female goes in search of comfortable creches in which to leave her eggs. She chooses other birds' nests which contain eggs of a similar colour to her own. She never leaves more than one egg per nest and sometimes even takes the precaution of eating one of her hosts' eggs, so that they won't notice the difference.

As soon as it hatches the cuckoo chick proves itself remarkably keen to evict its other nest-mates. This behaviour is thought to be driven by hyper-sensitive skin on its bare back, stimulating an ejection reflex in the cuckoo chick at the slightest contact. This reflex disappears when the chick's feathers grow at about four days old.

THE ANTISOCIAL CHICK: ME FIRST!

The female cuckoo has to lay quickly, while the nest's owners are away. She does not have time to enter their home and cannot take safety precautions. Luckily, the shell of her egg is strong enough to withstand the fall. The little cuckoo's head appears after an incubation period of 11 to 12 days. It usually hatches before the others in the nest. Immediately it sets about removing these potential rivals, throwing the eggs overboard. If, on hatching the cuckoo discovers another chick already in the nest, it behaves in exactly the same way. Very occasionally two cuckoos hatch at the

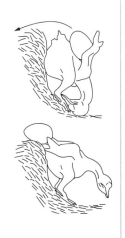
same time in the same nest, leading to a fratricidal duel. In the days immediately following the battle, the adoptive parents sit on the surviving chick to warm it. At four days old the young cuckoo starts to squawk for food and the devoted adults begin a constant round of trips to satisfy its hunger.

After many efforts the cuckoo has already done most of its work. It ceaselessly strives to throw eggs and chicks overboard until there are no others in the nest. Once alone with its new parents, this 'only child' can benefit from their undivided care and attention.

INSATIABLE APPETITE

The adoptive parents look after their little cuckoo with all the care they would have given to their own chick. Indeed, they show great devotion in trying to satisfy its insatiable appetite. This task takes all their time, for the little orphan eats as much as a brood of 4 or 5 of their own chicks. Gigantic meals take the cuckoo from 2.5 grammes to 75 grammes in two weeks. It reaches its adult weight in three weeks and, at 100 grammes, finds the little nest a bit of a squash.

The adult cuckoo is as greedy as its chick but, unlike its young, has to find its own food. Cuckoos show a clear preference for insects, particularly caterpillars. Next, in order of preference, come insect larvae, dung-beetles, scarabs, cockchafers and earthworms.

Profile

Common cuckoo
Cuculus canorus
Family: cuculidae
Class: birds

Wingspan: 55 – 60 cm
Weight: 100 – 130 g
Distribution: Europe, North Africa, Asia
Habitat: varied: woodland, bogs, marshes, steppes...
Diet: insects, preference for furry caterpillars
Incubation period: 11.5 days
Number of young: 8 – 12, in different nests
Egg weight: 3.5 g
Life expectancy: 12 years maximum
Sexual maturity: at 1 or 2 years

At two weeks old the young cuckoo is already much larger than its adoptive parents, who are often extremely careful when feeding their monster. What's more, the young cuckoo pecks them if it thinks the food is not coming fast enough.
Despite this bad treatment, the adults continue to take care of their burdensome parasite.

As soon as it can cry, the young cuckoo squawks for food with all its might.
It spends all day with its beak wide open, giving its devoted guardians the startling sight of its scarlet mouth.
This bright red signal stimulates its carers to increase the rate of feeds.

Ingenious and observant,
Japanese macaques
give each other recipes

FANS OF HEAT TREATMENT

In winter, the temperature on the high, snow-covered plateaux of Shiga, in Japan, often reaches −10°C. The macaque population that lives in this region has found a clever way of getting warm. Several times a day they visit the plateaux' hot springs and dive into the 40°C pools. For 5 to 10 minutes, the happy band snort and splash, then they get out of the water and shake themselves to dry their thick fur.

LOVERS OF GOOD FOOD

Biologists studying a group of macaques on the island of Koshima used to attract them by putting out sweet potatoes on a sandy beach. One day a young female dipped her potato in the seawater and rubbed it. Since then, this practice has spread throughout the entire troop and has been passed down to the younger generations, perhaps because they like the salty taste.

Profile

Japanese macaque
Macaca fuscata
Class: mammals
Order: primates

Size: 75 cm
Weight: male: 11 kg; female: 9 kg
Distribution: Japan
Habitat: broad-leaved and coniferous forest
Diet: primarily vegetarian (leaves, fruits), omnivorous (insects)
Number of young per litter: 1
Social structure: group with more than one male
Sexual maturity: 3.5 − 4 years

During the cold and snowy winters, the macaques of the Shiga plateaux gather near hot springs, drawn by the warm air rising from them. They are quick to swim across the pools, which act as vast hot-water bottles for the macaques.

The macaques of Japan live in wooded areas, where they find the leaves and fruits which make up most of their food. However, these monkeys are not afraid of water and some populations appreciate an opportunity to bathe.

Like all primates, macaques are very clever and curious. This young one, intrigued by the white blanket that has just covered the ground, is discovering all the properties of snow through play. Later he will be able to make great snowballs of more than 50 centimetres in diameter by rolling them along in front of him, so that he can play ball with the other young monkeys in his group.

In Shiga the winters are very hard.

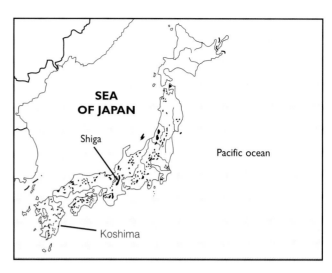
Distribution map of the Japanese macaque

FAMILY LIFE

The macaques of Japan live in groups organised around a few dominant adult males. When the group is on the move these males place themselves in the middle of the troop, surrounded by 'families' consisting of females with their young. The young males follow on the edge until they are strong enough to join one of the groups, or found one of their own.

Young macaques, too weak to travel on their own, never leave their mothers' sides.
They thus join in with all the activities of the group, learning all the actions that are essential for macaques.
They also bathe in pairs, though baths are more for warmth than grooming.

Sea otters live near the shore, but may go further out to sea. These champion swimmers have even been seen 15 kilometres from land. To rest they turn on to their backs and float.

To eat sea urchins
sea otters
use anvils

THE SEA'S TEETH

The sea otter loves to eat sea urchins, crabs, mussels and other animals with a protective shell. It is an excellent swimmer, diving as far as 30 metres down to collect its delicious meal of seafood on the rocky bottom. Once back on the surface, it lies on its back and cracks open the shells with its large, flat teeth. In California the sea otters are also known to bring up a pebble. On the surface they break the shells by knocking them on the stone which they place on their ribs to act as an anvil.

Sea otters seek out places sheltered from winds and currents. When they want to rest, they wind long brown seaweed around their bodies.

Profile

Sea otter
Enhydra lutris
Family: mustelidae
Class: mammals
Order: fissipedia

Size: 1.5 m (body and tail)
Weight: 30 – 40 kg
Distribution: North Pacific: California, Alaska, Aleutian Islands, Kamchatka, Kuril Islands
Habitat: sheltered coastlines where long seaweed (laminaria) are found
Diet: sea urchins, shellfish, molluscs, some fish
Number of young per litter: 1

This Californian sea otter is breaking a shell on a pebble that it has brought up from the sea bed. Otters may dive as deep as 60 metres and stay under water over five minutes. They swim by moving their hindquarters and feet from side to side, with their front feet against their chests.

With one beat of their wings
owl butterflies
frighten away their enemies

A TERRIFYING 'GLANCE'

The owl butterfly, or caligo, has no invincible shield or devastating weapon, and yet it manages to frighten its attackers away by means of a clever trick. Many birds like butterfly flesh and when they spot a caligo on a stem they move in to snap it up. If the butterfly, which keeps its wings folded when resting, becomes aware of danger, it quickly spreads its wings in front of its attacker, displaying a colourless screen from which two large open eyes seem to stare out, iridescent with sunlight. The surprised bird may pause in its attack for a second, giving the butterfly time to escape. A bird less easily influenced may try to attack these 'eyes' that have suddenly appeared. By drawing its aggressor's attention to this non-vital part of its body, the caligo may lose a piece of wing, but, crucially, saves its own life.

Profile

Owl butterfly
Caligo eurylachus
Class: insects
Order: lepidoptera

Wingspan: 10 – 15 cm
Distribution: tropical America
Habitat: the caligo reproduces on banana trees, whose leaves provide food for its larvae
Distinguishing mark: 'owl eye' design (called an ocellus) on the back of its hind wings
Active period: this butterfly flies in the early morning and in the late afternoon until dusk, avoiding the hottest sun

The owl butterfly lives in the tropical forests of Central and South America. Its larva, laid on the leaves of various species of banana, pupates into a chrysalis that looks like a dead leaf.

The designs on the owl butterfly's wings look surprisingly like eyes with dilated pupils. This disturbing 'look' can deter the boldest predators. In addition, the many scales which cover the wings are able to change their colour tones, giving an even more alarming effect.

With no tools but their teeth
beavers
build strong dams

In Alaska beavers' constructions can be very large.

RIVER ARCHITECT

Before setting to work, the beaver gauges the stream's rate of flow by listening to the sound of the water and swimming in the current. It chooses a place to build its dam according to the river's shape and the obstacles it contains, then it finds a place a little upstream and begins to cut down trees. It uses the current to transport its logs to a support it has identified in the stream, then places successive layers of logs and mud on the foundations of wood and stone, building up a dam.

A comfortable maisonette

The entrance to the beaver's hut or burrow is always in the water, from which a corridor leads to the dry part of the dwelling. The first level is at the opening of this tunnel and is used as a terrace for drying. The beaver has its bed on the upper floor, which it lines with wood shavings.

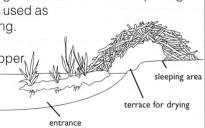

sleeping area

terrace for drying

entrance

To build their dams, beavers cut tree trunks into a point, using their sharp incisors. They cut up logs of similar weight, altering the length according to the diameter of the trunk.

This small tree will not withstand the beaver's sharp canines for much longer. Once the tree has been cut down, the rodent will feast on its leaves and young roots.

Beavers use the river current to transport their load down to the dam. These animal builders are able to grade the weight of their logs and use them according to size and shape to reinforce the weak parts of the dam. Their constructions play a part in limiting the rise in water levels by regulating the flow of mountain streams.

The European beaver's fur is not as silky as that of its American cousin. However both species have a long tail, broad and flat, which they use as a propeller when setting off or swimming quickly. For diving, this tail functions like an aeroplane's elevator.

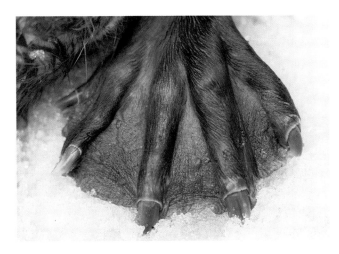

The beaver's hind feet are webbed.

Profile

American beaver
Castor canadensis
Family: castoridae
Class: mammals
Order: rodents
Size: head and body:
60 – 80 cm; tail: 25 – 45 cm long and
11 – 18 cm wide
Weight: 12 – 25 kg; 40 kg; females are often
heavier
Distribution: North America, from Alaska to
northern Mexico
Habitat: large regions of open woodland
near water
Diet: strictly herbivorous (leaves,
roots, bark)

LIVING IN AN ARTIFICIAL LAKE

The beaver builds a dam in order to exploit its reservoir. First, it makes an underwater entrance to its hut or nest so that it will be hidden and inaccessible to predators. Then it stockpiles its food at the bottom of the 'swimming pool' in readiness for winter scarcity, since the beaver, which feeds only on leaves, bark and branches, cannot gather these when they are covered in snow. So during the warm months it cuts up the trunks of young birches, willows, maples and poplars, and drags them to the bottom of the water, securing them with stones. In this way it has direct access from its hut through to its reservoir-cum-larder, without having to leave the water. This is a very convenient arrangement when a thick layer of ice forms on the surface of its lake in winter, preventing the beaver from going out into the open air. Thanks to its thick, waterproof fur, the beaver is not bothered by the water temperature, which is close to 0°C.

In summer, the beaver also eats plants that grow on the ground or in water, such as water-lilies, duckweed and pondweed.

Improving on nature

The beaver builds its hut and amenities in a wooded area. It starts by blocking off a river to create a reservoir, then it builds its hut, or settles for digging a burrow. All the building materials it needs come from the felling area in the neighbouring forest. The beaver puts the finishing touches to its residence by lining the reservoir with wood and installing a refectory.

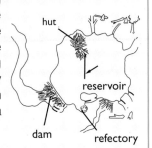

hut

reservoir

dam

refectory

Unique among birds
dippers
walk on the river bed

The dipper, which can be recognised by its white breast, can also be identified by the places it likes to frequent: cold and fast-flowing rivers. Perched on a vantage point, it scrutinises the swirling water, looking for insect larvae. Just before it dives, the bird performs ritual movements, moving up and down on its perch, like an athlete warming up.

THE BIRD THAT FEEDS UNDERWATER

The dipper lives on river banks in the mountainous regions of Europe, central Asia and Alaska. To feed, it flies over a fast-flowing stream in search of a rock sticking out of the water, on which it stands. After flexing its legs a few times it suddenly dives under the water. By flapping its wings it reaches the bottom, where it clings to the stones with its long claws, using its tail and wings for balance. It walks upstream underwater, digging around in plant waste and under stones, looking for insect larvae.

The bird suddenly leaps under the water. It immediately reaches the bottom, swimming against the current by beating its wings. Its feathers slide through the water without getting wet. On dry land the bird waterproofs and preens its tight plumage, greasing it with secretions from its uropygial gland, located near the base of its tail.

Closely associated with mountain torrents, the dipper is the only truly aquatic passerine. It spends its days by fast-flowing streams, moving upstream after each dive. Thus, both from the air and underwater, it explores the areas where its food, aquatic larvae, grow and develop.

Our brilliant aquatic cousin
the dolphin
isn't big headed!

REMARKABLE ABILITIES

Dolphins have a reputation for being extremely intelligent. Scientists have carried out comparative intelligence tests on different species of mammals using the encephalisation quotient (EQ), which is obtained by dividing brain volume by the animal's surface area. The higher the EQ, the higher the intellectual capacities of the animal. For example, the EQ of human beings is 7.4 and that of chimpanzees is 2.5. The EQ figure for the bottle-nosed dolphin is 5.6.

According to this scientific approach, the large brain-size of the dolphin will allow it to carry out specific tasks. For example, these animals can communicate using a 'vocabulary' and complex bodily positions, enabling them to live in groups. In addition, when they have just given birth, the females whistle all day long and their young, who have exceptional learning abilities, soon learn to recognise their mother's voice.

Profile

Bottle-nosed dolphin
Tursiops truncatus
Class: mammals
Order: odontoceti

Size: male: up to 3.9 m
Weight: male: 275 kg; female lighter
Distribution: all seas
Habitat: coastal waters and open sea
Diet: carnivorous
Number of young per litter:
1 every 2 or 3 years
Social structure: lives in groups;
10 individuals for coastal animals,
25 for ocean dolphins (on average)

Curious and fearless, this bottle-nosed dolphin puts its head out of the water to observe events on the surface. Due to a particularity of its eyes, it can see well in both water and air. When it moves from water to air, or vice versa, the shape of its crystalline lens alters slightly.

For play, communication or simply to go faster, dolphins can perform aerial acrobatics. These common dolphins are leaping out of the water using a ship's bow wave. They can take advantage of this current to follow vessels over long distances, to the great satisfaction of the passengers.

The learning capacities and exceptional skill of dolphins have gained them much human admiration. When kept in captivity in marine zoos, they are trained to perform leaps and to beat their tails. The shows attract a great number of tourists, who are fascinated by such acrobatic turns, to the detriment of the animal, which gets bored in these confined spaces.

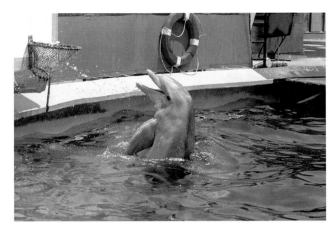

The dolphin's abilities are used for human entertainment.

Dolphin radar

To locate itself, the dolphin has a kind of radar. Its frontal bump gives out sounds which spread out in front of it. When they meet an obstacle, these waves are reflected and return to the dolphin. This echo is caught in the animal's lower jaw and transmitted to its brain, where it is analysed to provide an image of the shape of the objects encountered.

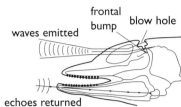

LIKE A FISH IN WATER

The dolphin, whose ancestors once lived on dry land, is a mammal which is now perfectly adapted to living in water. Its powerful tail, elongated shape and very supple skin enable it to reach great speeds.

It thus manages to follow boats with remarkable ease and even surfs on the bow wave, performing amazing glides. It seems to like the presence of human beings, whom it accompanies on deep-sea dives and, sometimes, may even save from drowning.

In their groups, dolphins spend a lot of time playing. They like to caress each other and exchange friendly nudges; young males particularly enjoy contact with young females. These games bind the group together and educate the younger ones in the rudiments of dolphin life.

When danger threatens
hedgehogs
curl into a ball

When the hedgehog is walking, only its face is vulnerable. Protected by its armour of spines, the hedgehog does not fear many predators. Its defences are completed by a resistance to poisons, such as the venom of the viper or the sting of the bee.

IT ROLLS INTO A BALL AND BRISTLES

Small, fairly slow-moving and unable to fly or jump, the hedgehog would be an ideal prey were it not covered in prickles. Its first reaction when it feels threatened is to flee. However, if it cannot get away from its attacker on its short legs, it stops and takes up a defensive posture.

It draws in its shoulders, lowers its face and makes the prickles on its forehead stand on end. This deters most animals from trying to attack. If the threat continues, the hedgehog bends its legs and rolls into a ball.

During this transformation small muscles push the hedgehog's head and the hind part of its body against its belly. At the same time, the skin on its back stretches around its body like a bag

The hedgehog spends the day under a tree-stump or in a dense thicket, alone in the shelter it has made comfortable with dead leaves and dried grass. It only comes out at night fall, going in search of food, which it locates using its senses of smell and hearing.

Baby hedgehogs feed by suckling from their mother.

containing the head, feet and tail. To complete its defences, small muscles at the base of the spines contract, making the animal look like an uninviting ball of needles.

AN OPPORTUNISTIC HUNTER

The hedgehog likes to hide and waits until nightfall before leaving its shelter of leaves. Guided by sound and smell, it makes for gardens, undergrowth or the hedges around cultivated fields in order to hunt its food. It pokes its nose into tufts of grass and moss, dead leaves and clods of earth, preferring damp places.

If, during this search, an earthworm emerges or a beetle wanders in the moonlight, the hedgehog snaps it up with its sharp little teeth. It prefers to eat animals that are easy to catch, but will also devour caterpillars, centipedes, spiders and frogs, if they are not too lively and quick.

A prickly ball

The hedgehog uses a number of special muscles to adopt its defensive 'ball' position. First the small muscles in the skin of its head and the hind part of its body tighten, stretching the broad caudo-dorsal muscle right round the body. Then the orbicular muscle, which surrounds the animal's back when it is resting, contracts, enclosing the head and legs in a 'bag' of prickles.

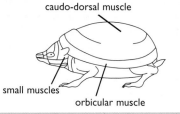

caudo-dorsal muscle

small muscles

orbicular muscle

The adult hedgehog is covered in almost 5000 spines; when it rolls into a ball it makes them stand up in all directions and can stay like that for hours, safe from all danger.

Farmers, breeders, tailors and architects,
ants
are the most gifted of insects

In the tropical and subtropical forests of America, fungus-culturing ants are cutting leaves. The leaves bear the indelible marks of the damage caused by the ants and are a sure sign of a nearby ants' nest.

LEAF CUTTERS

Leaf-cutting ants are the true farmers of the miniature world. They have mastered every part of fungus production. To feed the growing fungi, the colony's worker ants cut pieces of leaf, which they bring to the nest for treatment. The leaves are then chewed, treated and placed in the fungus nursery. The ants regularly maintain 'fields', where they put substances that aid the decomposition of vegetable matter and are useful as fertiliser. At 'harvest' time, the worker ants collect little balls of fungus, which they distribute in the colony.

Ants transport pieces of leaf cut into rounded shapes from the collection site to the fungus-growing area, where they will be treated. The large worker ants, responsible for cutting tand transporting the leaf pieces, are accompanied by smaller lookouts whose job is to ensure that parasitic flies do not attack the colony (top left, a lookout on guard, perched on a piece of leaf).

Various vegetable elements are used by the fungus-growers.

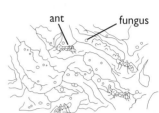
THE QUEEN'S FUNGI

When a queen leaves her nest to go and set up a new colony, she takes with her a fragment of fungus. When she arrives at her new nesting site, she spits her starter fungus into a small hole and starts to lay eggs.

When they hatch, the first worker ants start to build a fungus-field and supply it with leaf fragments. They work so effectively that their monoculture can feed up to a million worker ants and larvae.

The fungus-growing ants, which specialise in leaf-cutting, are equipped with sharp, powerful mandibles which slice through the leaves. They hold the cut piece with their six legs, while their mouthpieces work through the vegetable matter. While performing this task, they pivot around on one spot to cut out rounded pieces.

When they find a group of aphids, the herding ants take them under their protection. They then drive their flock to tender stems, where the aphids can find abundant food. If a ladybird approaches, the ants drive it away.

These red ants take good care of their charges, constantly checking that they are protected from predators, have all the sap they need and do not escape the ants' vigilance. Not content with gathering and guiding their aphids, the guards also warn their flock of an enemy's presence.

WEAVER ANTS

In Africa and Asia ants build delicate little nests by rolling up the leaves of trees. In the forest large worker ants identify the ideal leaves, then grasp their edges with their mandibles and their legs and pull them together. The small workers find larvae in an old nest and use them as sewing machines: after stimulation, the larvae produce silk threads which the workers use to sew the two edges of a leaf together.

HERDING ANTS

Some ants cannot draw sap from plants, although sap is the basis of their diet. Aphids feed on sap, however, by sucking it up using their proboscis, which they plunge into the stems. They only absorb part of the sugary liquid, expelling the rest, which is called honeydew and which red ants love to eat. Some have the job of finding aphid colonies, which are then

Ants and aphids

Zoological research has shown that the hind part of some aphids is similar in shape to the head of an ant. Since ants swap food by regurgitation, scientists have developed a theory of the relationship between ants and aphids according to which milking ants confuse ants with aphids, requesting food from the latter as they would from a fellow ant.

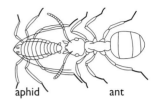

aphid   ant

husbanded in herds, like domestic animals. A milking ant frequently approaches one of the aphids, tickling it with its antennae. The aphid reacts to this stimulation by lifting its abdomen and excreting a tiny drop of honeydew through its anus. The ant then swallows the delicious liquid and stores it in its crop so it can be delivered to its fellow ants. In exchange for the gift of food, the ants defend the aphids against their enemies, the ladybirds.

The aphid willingly collaborates with the ant, which stimulates it with its antennae. The aphid raises its abdomen and expels a drop of honeydew, which is licked up by the ant that is caressing it. Milking is a delicate operation, since ladybirds and other aphid predators take advantage of the ant's inattention to attack the herd.

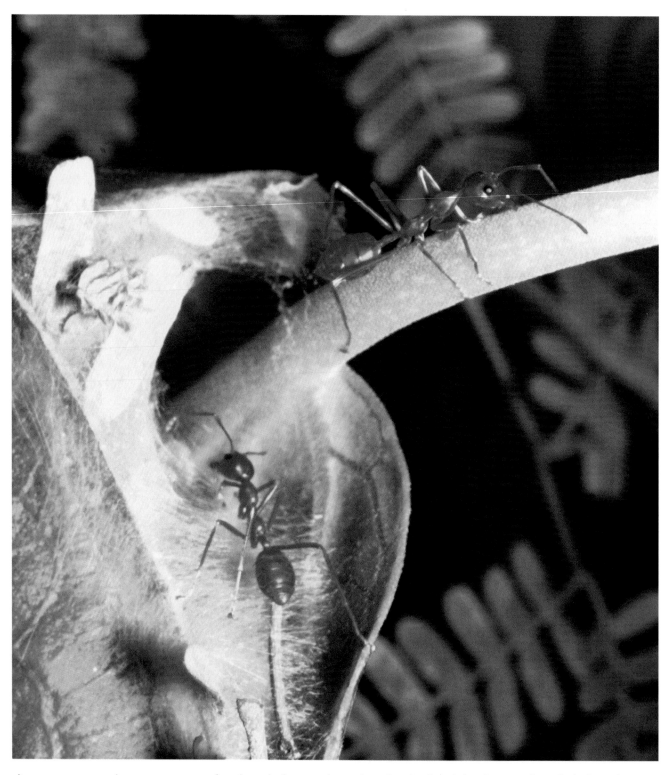

Among weaver ants there are two types of workers: the large workers, whose function is to bring the two edges of a leaf together, and the small workers, which 'sew' the leaves up, using larvae which they hold between their mandibles.
These two castes differ in both their size and the tasks they perform.

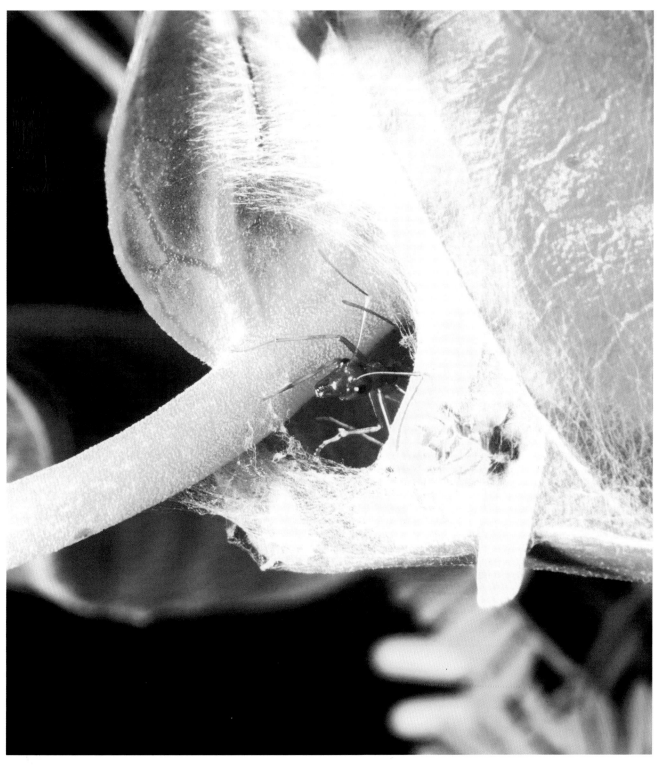

Weaver ants are highly territorial and fiercely defend their nests against intrusion by other insects. This aggressiveness is well known to human beings who, in some countries, have developed ant husbandry, placing the ants next to their cultivated fields. In this way their crops are protected against the ravages of some types of insect without need of insecticide.

Egyptian vultures
use a hammer to eat eggs

The Egyptian vulture's face is featherless.

The Egyptian vulture takes long glides through the air, carefully studying the ground in search of a dead body or some other prey. Its small size enables it to perform aerial acrobatics and to fly along beating its wings, which is much more tiring for the larger species.

SMALL BEAK, BIG APPETITE

Gliding through the air, the Egyptian vulture studies the ground, looking for carrion. Its beak is not very strong and does not permit it to take on tough carcasses. When a large mammal dies, the Egyptian vulture waits, during which time larger vultures pull the animal to pieces. When the more powerful creatures have had their fill, the Egyptian vulture approaches cautiously and, using its long, thin beak, takes scraps of flesh that were inaccessible to the larger birds.

The Egyptian vulture does not only clean large carcasses, it also eats all kinds of reptiles, birds and small mammals, as long as they are dead or dying. Sometimes it even eats the insect larvae that develop in rotting flesh.

The Egyptian vulture is not a very sociable bird, but it will accept the company of its fellows on rare occasions, when feeding or resting. It sometimes mingles with groups of vultures of larger species, hoping for some of the remains of a large carcase.

EGGS ON THE MENU

Some Egyptian vultures supplement their diet with a few eggs. To eat a small egg, like that of a pelican, the vulture picks it up in its beak and breaks it open by dropping it on a rock. With a larger, stronger egg, such as that of an ostrich, it uses a different technique. It selects a stone weighing less than 1 kilogram, picks it up in its beak and holds its head above the egg, then throws its tool down on the shell, repeating the operation until the target cracks. It then pokes its narrow beak into the hole and feasts on the contents.

CUNNING AND DETERMINED

The Egyptian vulture is among the ten or so bird species that manipulate objects with their beaks for use as a tool. Some indefatigable Egyptian vultures have been known to spend over an hour trying to get into an artificial egg!
However, only a few sedentary percnopteri eat birds' eggs, which sugests that this behaviour is learned rather than innate.

Despite its dishevelled appearance, the Egyptian vulture takes great care of its plumage. After plunging its head and feathers in an animal's rotting innards, it dries itself in the sun.

A young Egyptian vulture with immature plumage gets to grips with an egg. The difficult thing is to lift the head high enough while keeping an eye on the target in order to aim.

Profile

Egyptian vulture
Neophron percnopterus
Class: birds
Order: falconiformes

Size: wingspan of 1.55 – 1.8 m
Weight: 2 kg (average)
Habitat: open areas of scattered vegetation including mountains
Diet: corpses, detritus, excrement
Number of eggs: 1 – 3 (usually 2)
Life expectancy: about 20 years
Social structure: monogamous, sometimes gregarious

The horned toad takes its name from its two 'eyeshades'.

As soon as the horned toad leaves its hiding-place in the leaves or mud, it becomes easy to see. Insects, lizards and frogs which suddenly find themselves staring at this solid body and large, powerful jaws get away as quickly as they can.

When camouflaged, some
animals
look like plants

KILLER LURKING IN THE MUD

Crouching under a pile of dead leaves or in a muddy puddle, the horned toad patiently waits for a lizard or small frog to pass close enough to be caught and eaten. The toad's warty skin, speckled with green and brown, provides a perfect camouflage in the Brazilian forest.

THE BRANCH THAT BLINKS

This tawny frogmouth lives in wooded regions of Australia. So that its enemies cannot see it, it spends its days perching on a branch. Its grey plumage with dark stripes perfectly imitates the appearance of its perch. The bird even stretches out its neck to look like a branch.

With its camouflage, the horned toad goes unnoticed on the forest floor. In this way it lies in wait for small animals, jumping on them when they pass within reach of its jaws. This toad, which may be up to 20 centimetres long, is voracious and extremely aggressive towards potential victims, even those of its own size.

This Australian tawny frogmouth has small feathers above its eyes which hide the featherless part of its beak. When the bird senses it has been seen, it leaves its camouflage position and fluffs out its feathers to intimidate its enemy.

This tawny frogmouth can stay entirely motionless on a branch for hours on end. It chooses a tree of a similar colour to its own plumage and adopts its camouflage position. To do this, it stretches out its neck, points its beak to the sky, and almost entirely closes its eyes, keeping only a tiny crack open to observe its surroundings.

The wings of Kallima butterflies can change colour.

LICHEN SWALLOWS FLIES

The Madagascan flat-tailed gecko wins the prize for the best imitative disguise. Every part of its body looks like tufts of the lichen that grows on the trees where its spends its time. The irregular brown stripes decorating its skin and the fringes scattered over its body help to make it invisible to its predators. The gecko also exploits these attributes to catch incautious insects.

DEAD LEAVES THAT FLY AWAY

Kallima butterflies, common in India and Australia, look as though they are using two leaves for wings. When they rest on dead leaves they go unnoticed. For these insects, which do not have weapons like stings or strong jaws, camouflage provides good protection.

The designs on the Kallima butterflies' wings look like leaf veins. The small markings even look like the spots that appear on leaves when they are ready to fall. The butterfly's camouflage, which is very effective on a background of dead vegetation, becomes a handicap when it ventures into green, lush surroundings.

The flat-tailed gecko is a good climber thanks to the suckers it has under its toes.
In the forests of the island of Madagascar it climbs into the trees to hide among the lichens and mosses,
keeping still so that it does not to draw the attention of other animals.

Creative workshop

*Having studied all of these creatures,
it's time to get creative.*

*All you need are a few odds and ends and a little ingenuity,
and you can incorporate some of the animals we've seen
into beautiful craft objects.*

*These simple projects will give you further insight into the
animal kingdom presented in the pages of this book.*

*An original and simple way to enjoy
the wonderful images of the animal kingdom.*

Penguin shirt

Page 84

Pelican clock

Page 86

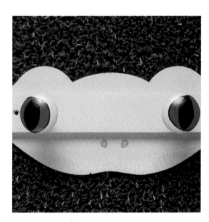

Frog clothes peg

Page 88

Bee hairband and hairslide

Page 90

Penguin shirt

*D*ecorate a plain white shirt with this striking penguin design.

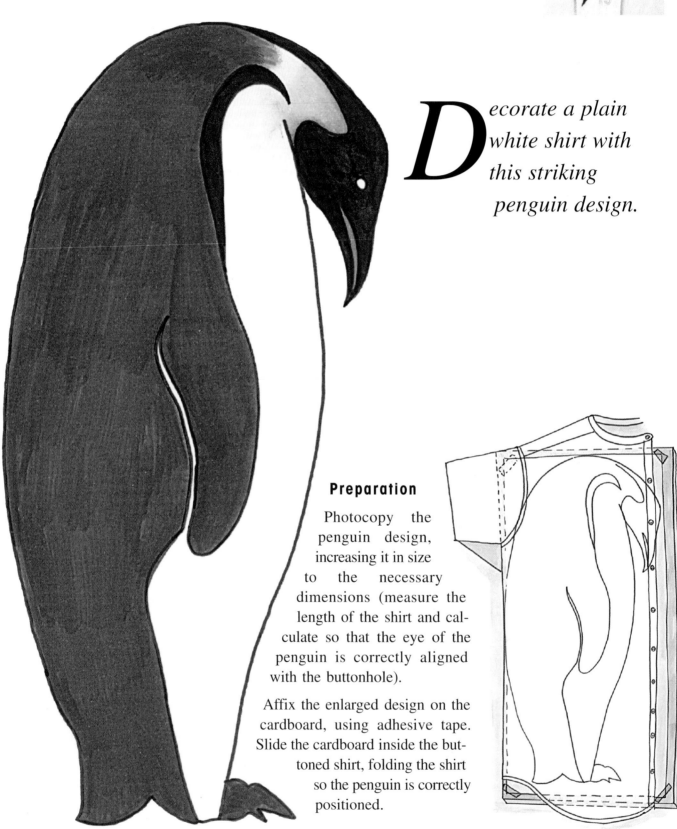

Preparation

Photocopy the penguin design, increasing it in size to the necessary dimensions (measure the length of the shirt and calculate so that the eye of the penguin is correctly aligned with the buttonhole).

Affix the enlarged design on the cardboard, using adhesive tape. Slide the cardboard inside the buttoned shirt, folding the shirt so the penguin is correctly positioned.

Painting

Use the medium paintbrush and black fabric paint to draw the outline of the penguin. Fill in the penguin's head and the wing with the black paint.

Dilute the black paint a little and use this paint to complete the body and the foot. The body will then be slightly paler than the wing.

Use the red paint to colour the beak and the edge of the head.

Paint yellow paint on to these two areas quickly so the paint mixes to make an uneven orange.

Finishing

Allow the paint to dry. Turn the shirt over and iron it on the back for a few minutes, without steam, to fix the paint.

Remove the button where the eye will be and replace it with the 'eye button'.

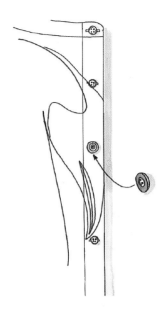

Materials

• a plain white cotton shirt • fabric paint in black, red and yellow • a decorative button resembling an eye • a sheet of thin cardboard the same size as the shirt • adhesive tape • a large paintbrush and a medium paintbrush • an iron

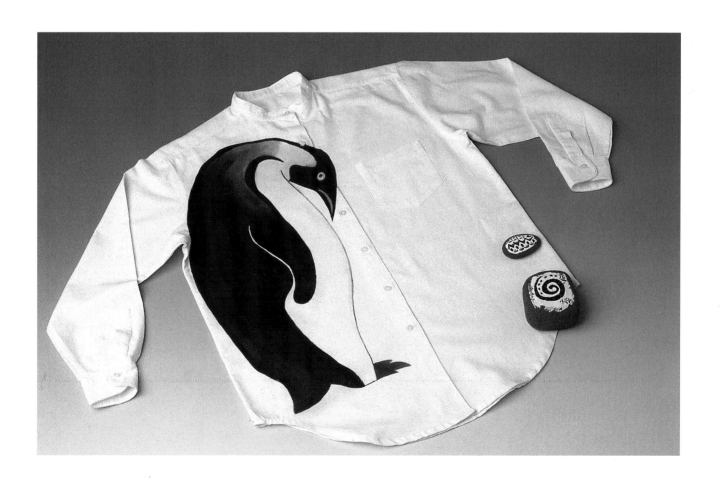

Pelican clock

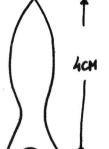

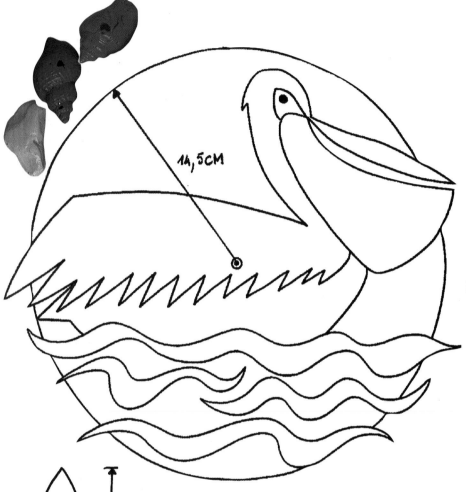

14,5CM

*T*his beady-eyed pelican may be eating the blue fish, but he's still got his eye on the orange fish as time ticks past.

4CM

Cutting out the pelican and the pieces

Photocopy the designs, increasing them to the size required.

Place the photocopy of the pelican on the thin cardboard and attach the corners with adhesive tape.

Cut out the pelican in two pieces, the four waves, the two sections of the beak and a fish.

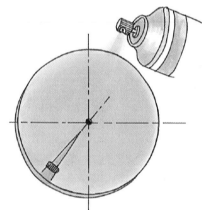

Making up the background of the clock

Trace a circle 29 centimetres in diameter on to the thick cardboard and cut it out using the Stanley knife.

Pierce a hole in the centre large enough to affix the clock mechanism.

Paint the circular piece of cardboard using the blue spray paint, then use the white paint to give the effect of clouds.

Decorating the pieces

Allow the paint to dry. Glue the thin cardboard shapes on to the background, placing the blue fish in the pelican's beak. Pierce the thin cardboard in the centre. Make shells or starfish to stick among the waves if you wish.

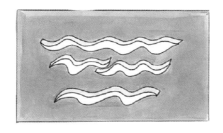

Connecting the clock mechanism

Follow the manufacturer's instructions to attach the mechanism.

Second-hand

Cut a fish out of orange paper. Paint the second hand orange. Once the paint is dry, stick the fish on to it.

Materials

• a sheet of thin cardboard • a piece of thick cardboard 30 centimetres square
• coloured paper, in blue and orange • a clock mechanism with three hands • a can of pale blue spray paint, a can of white spray paint and some orange acrylic paint • strong liquid glue •adhesive tape• a Stanley knife
• a small paintbrush
• a sharp instrument to pierce the cardboard
• a compass for drawing a circle

Frog clothes peg

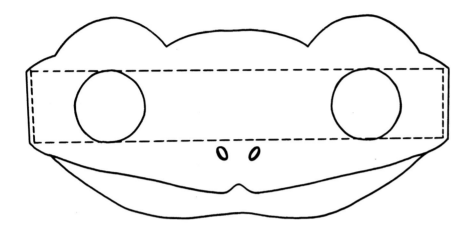

*S*traight out of the Amazonian forest, this green creature makes himself useful.

The shape of the frog

Photocopy the design, increasing it to the necessary size (slightly larger than the piece of wood).

Put the photocopy on the sheet of plywood, affixing it with adhesive tape. Cut two pieces with the Stanley knife.

Sand the edges of the frog shapes.

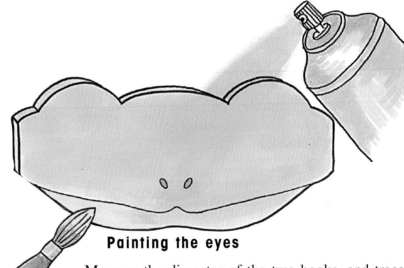

Painting the eyes

Measure the diameter of the two hooks, and trace a circle of this diameter on to a piece of paper using the compass. Also trace two circles of a slightly larger diameter. Overlap the two larger circles, so that the overlap forms the shape of the pupil. The pupil will be the height of the smaller circle.

Using the three circles as a template, put them under the transparent adhesive paper and cut out two stencils, one for the red and one for the black pupil. Place the first stencil over the first hook and use the red paint to cover the surface. Remove the stencil carefully. Repeat the process for the other hook.

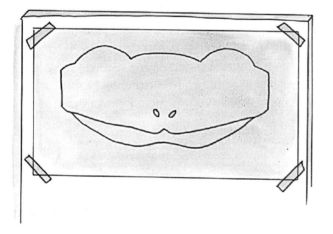

Allow to dry, then place the second stencil on the hook and use black paint to form the pupil.

Preparing the wood

Spread a layer of plaster of Paris on the piece of wood with the brush. Once it has dried, sand it to give a smooth surface. Spray with green paint.

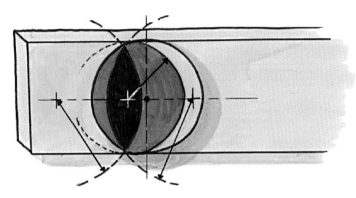

Painting the head and assembly of the coat hook

Spray the plywood shape green as shown, not forgetting the edges.

Allow to dry. Use a paintbrush to paint the mouth yellow and the nostrils dark green.

Once the paint has dried, glue the piece of wood on to the frog.

Pierce the plywood where the two coat hooks are affixed.

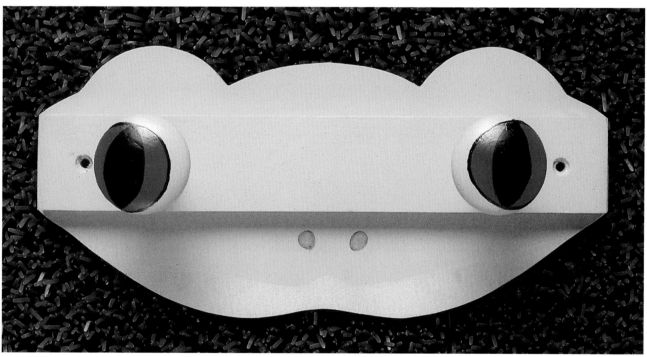

Materials

• a piece of wood with two round clothes pegs • a piece of thin plywood or thick cardboard (2 millimetres thick) • cans of acrylic spraypaint in yellow, black, and dark green • adhesive tape • transparent adhesive paper • very strong glue • a medium paintbrush and a thin paintbrush • a Stanley knife • a compass • fine sandpaper • a brush • plaster of Paris • an awl.

Bee hairband and hairslide

*L*ike bees to honey! Wear these beautiful felt bees in your hair.

Preparing the hairslide

Glue the green felt around the hairslide. Trim the edges, so they can not be seen

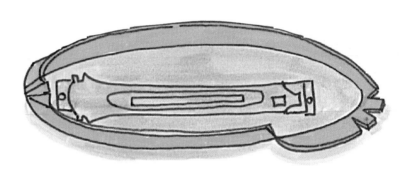

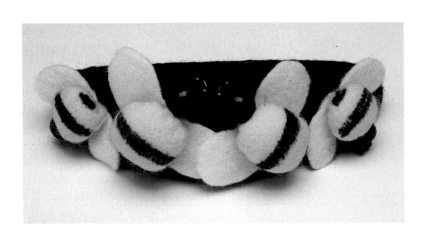

For each bee cut out a circle of yellow felt, approximately 3.5 centimetres in diameter. Sew around the edge of the circle using running stitch, place a small ball of kapok in the centre, and pull the thread tight. Knot the thread, but do not cut.

Making the bees

Cut a wing piece from the white felt. You will need about four bees on the hairslide and five on the hairband.

Place the yellow ball on the middle of the white shape, with the sewn edge at the bottom. Sew into place.

At the front end, thread one large bead, then two smaller ones on to the thread. Take the thread back through the large bead, arrange the smaller beads as eyes, and fasten off the thread.

Using the fabric pen, draw black lines across the yellow body of the bee.

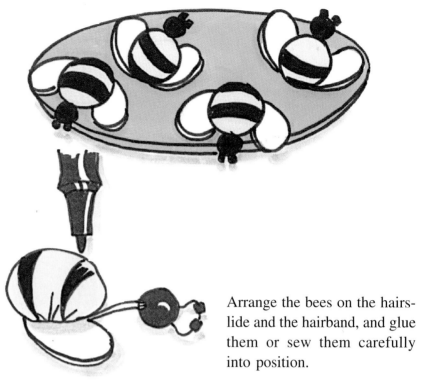

Arrange the bees on the hairslide and the hairband, and glue them or sew them carefully into position.

Materials

• pieces of green, yellow and white felt • plastic hairslide
• fabric-covered hairband
• fabric glue • tracing paper (for pattern) • yellow thread
• a small amount of kapok
• small and large black beads • black fabric pen

Photographic credits

Colibri: G. Abadie: 47, 48; Baranger : 62b; A. Christof: 77b; P. Etcheverry: 57; J.H. Maraindaz: 72b;
C. Ratier: 20c; A. Saunier: 17; F. et J.L. Ziegler: 52a

Nature: Anagnostidis: 16a, 43; D.S. Berthon: 76c; Franco Bonnard: 16c; Hervé Chaumeton: 22a, 22b, 22c, 23a, 23b, 23c, 39,
40b, 41a, 44b, 45, 67a, 74, 75; Chaumeton/Lanceau: 30c, 36a, 37a, 41b, 42a, 42b, 69b; Delacour: 14b; Ferrero: 32a, 34a, 79b;
Gohier: 37b, 54a, 54b, 64-65, 65, 70b, 71a; Grospas: 33b, 35, 70a, 80a; Krasnodebski: 58b, 69a; Lanceau: 14a, 40a, 67b, 79a;
Mayet: 30a, 30b, 31, 38-39, 68a; P. Meitz: 12; Polking: 32b, 33a, 80b; Reille: 34b;
Dr. Frieder Sauer: 15, 24-25a, 49, 71b, 76a, 76b, 77a; R. Siegel: 68b;

Okapia: Hansgeorg Arndt: 61b; Bildarchiv: 58c; Joe Mc Donald: 10-11, 78a; Jett Foot: 28; Helmut Göthel: 44a; Dr. Eckart Pott: 8b, 58a; Hans
Reinhard: 7b, 60, 61a; Nils Reinhard: 20b, 36b; W. Rohdich: 78c; Bruno Roth: 46b; Anup Shah: 20a

Phone: Auscape International/Jean-Paul Ferrero: 50-51, 53a, 53b, 78b; Collection " J ": 46a; J.P. Ferrero/J.M. Labat: 21;
Pascal Goetgheluck: 25b, 56-57, 73; François Gohier: 26a, 26b, 27, 29, 52b, 55; Hautala Hannu: 59;
J.F. Hellio/N. Van Ingen: 11, 13, 16b, 62a, 63; Jean-Michel Labat: 18b-19b; Labat/Jardel: 81;
Patrice Olivier: 72a: G. Robertson/Auscape; 6a, 6b, 7a, 8a, 9

Acknowledgements

The publishers would like to thank all those who have contributed to this book, in particular:
Antoine Caron, Michèle Forest, Nicolas Lemaire, Hervé Levano, Kha Luan Pham,
Vincent Pompougnac, Marie-Laure Sers-Besson, Emmanuelle Zumstein

Illustration: Franz Rey
Translation: Trista Selous for Ros Schwartz Translations - London, Sarah Snake

Printing: Eurolitho - Milan
Dépôt légal September 1998
Printed in Italy